# French Chic Beauty: The French Beauty Bible

# The French Chic Series

## Veronique Blanchard

# Table of Contents

# Introduction

Let me start by telling you something very important. Whether someone else has said this to you or not, trust me on it: You are beautiful! I urge you to drop your judgments and self-criticism to embrace your perfection.

When you begin to love yourself for who you are and embrace your true self without judgments, you automatically become the most mesmerizingly attractive version of yourself. Use this book as a guide to bring out the best in you but always remember: You are beautiful and perfect exactly the way you are!

In my first two books, *French Chic: The Ultimate Guide to French Fashion, Beauty and Style* and *French Chic Living: The Ultimate Guide to a Life of Elegance, Beauty and Style*, I shared with you how my mother's impeccable sense of style and aesthetics has had a powerful impact on my life. I also discussed how the years that I spent living in the US gave me a strong idea of the contrasts that exist between the two cultures while helping me comprehend why almost everyone seems to be fascinated by the French way of life.

Ultimately, this knowledge and understanding became my inspiration for creating the French Chic series. If you have read the first two books, then you already know that the first book was primarily a guide to dressing like a French woman and the second was all about adopting French Chic as a lifestyle.

I regularly receive requests from a lot of readers to share more of the 'insider secrets' that I have learned and acquired through my French upbringing. I find it quite intriguing just how insatiable the hunger for French Chic really is. I consider myself truly blessed to be in a position to bring value to so many people around the world by means of sharing my knowledge.

Since I'm still amazed by how well put-together Maman (my mother) always looked no matter how much she had on her platter (considering it's no easy business handling a household of four), it seems only natural to make this book all about the beauty secrets of French women.

In this book, I'll share with you all the beauty secrets I personally incorporate into my daily life. Beauty is a lifestyle in France so the tips presented in this book will cover all aspects of feeling and looking your best every day. We'll cover a wide range of topics including but not limited to cultivating the beauty mindset, building a beauty schedule, wardrobe care, skin, nail, and hair care tips.

I have said it in my previous books and I'll say it again – Since all the information presented in this book comes from my own experiences, you can trust that they really work.

I have chosen to keep this book very practical and fluff-free so that you can get maximum value out of it with a minimum investment of your time. Each chapter is densely packed with important information and tips for applying it in your life.

Don't just read this book but turn it into a way of life. I'm very sure that if you do everything, or at least, some of the things I have shared in this book, then you will surely become the cynosure of all eyes wherever you go.

I would suggest that you keep this book as a reference guide and regularly keep coming back to it for inspiration. You might not be able to apply all the ideas presented here instantly, but over time, doing one thing at a time, you'd be able to build a schedule that keeps you looking and feeling your best at all times.

Without further adieu, let's initiate you into the secrets of French beauty care.

# Chapter 1

# Practical Tips to Enhance Your Inner Beauty

**How you feel inside determines how good you'll look outside. In this chapter, we'll discuss practical tips that will enable your inner beauty to shine through your outer persona.**

Have you ever noticed how when you feel you are looking great, the whole world seems to agree with you? On the other hand, when you wake up feeling less than fabulous, you get treated the same way by others. Believe it or not, your outer reality is only a reflection of your inner reality.

If you want other people to treat you like you were the most amazing woman in the world, then you must first feel that way within. This doesn't make you self-centered or egoistic as you are not competing with anyone else. You only strive to be better than who you were yesterday and to be the finest most fabulous version of yourself day in and day out.

Therefore, being the chicest version of yourself requires caring for yourself on both the inside and the outside. No matter what anyone else says, a healthy sense of self-solve will not make you self-centered. Instead, it will make you indestructible as being fully immersed in self-love takes away the need to seek acceptance and praise from others. At the same time, you don't become flummoxed or start doubting yourself if someone criticizes you.

In this chapter, I am going to give you a few practices that you can incorporate into your daily life. This is your program for inner beautification. The beauty of your soul will always shine through your face. Taking the time to care for your soul is necessary for becoming the best and most fabulous version of yourself.

## Wake Up with Gratitude

Gratitude is the most powerful form of prayer. Whatever you are grateful for will always multiply in your life. If you want to have a blessed life, then make it a point to start and end your day with gratitude. I personally like to keep a gratitude journal in which I write down 5 things that I am grateful for every day.

The challenge here is to come up with something new every day – this way you are not taking anything in your life for granted. I also like to include at least 3 small things in this list. Something like having an arm can easily be taken for granted or even having makeup brushes for that matter. You might even find it silly to include things like these but by including the smallest of things in your gratitude list, you will begin to see real magic unfold in your life.

Also, if you really think these things are small, then imagine what it must be like to live without an arm or having to apply your makeup without makeup brushes! The beauty of life lies in the fact that every little piece of the puzzle is necessary to make our life complete.

I would suggest that you do this practice right after waking up. Keep the journal next to your bed and as soon as you wake up, instead of jumping out of bed in a reactionary mode, start your day with love and gratitude for all the blessings that you already have in your life.

Doing this simple practice with sincerity every day will help you more at peace with yourself and your life. When you become peaceful and content, you become chicer.

## End Your Day with Gratitude

Write down 5 things that happened in your day for which you are really grateful. They can be big or small things. The only thing that matters is that you should be feeling grateful from the core of your heart.

If you had a particularly challenging day and feel like there was absolutely nothing to be grateful for on that day, even then make an effort to be grateful. This practice is about elevating your mood and, thereby, the overall quality of your life.

Don't forget that even if you think that there is nothing good in your life, someone else might be looking at your life and thinking, "If only I could be her and have her life, how happy I'd be." Even if you think there is nothing good in your day, at least you have a nice warm bed to sleep on. At least, you have hands and feet, or, at least, you could afford to buy food. If you think about it, there are a million things to be grateful for. You could even be grateful for the fact that you are reading this book.

While doing this practice, always remember that you are not doing this because you are noble or nice, you are doing this because you want to experience the highest quality of life possible and to be the finest most incredible version of yourself.

If you do these two practices for a month, then I can promise you that you will start experiencing miracles in your life. Just make sure that you are doing this practice with passion and emotions. Don't make it a mechanical process. Emotions are your power – the more strongly you feel about something, the more that thing will increase in your life.

**Beauty Affirmations**

Include 1-2 affirmations in your daily journal. In case you are not familiar with what an affirmation is, then let me define it for you. Affirmations are positive statements written in the present tense that are meant to foster your belief in a positive idea which, in turn, will lead to greater self-empowerment and self-confidence.

Every day, choose one or two affirmations and write them down in your journal at the start of the day. I would suggest that you create your own affirmations so that you have a strong emotional connection with the words.

Here are a few examples:

*"I am gorgeous. I am beautiful. I love myself unconditionally."*

*"I have a perfect body. I love my body unconditionally."*

*"The perfection of my soul is perfectly represented in the perfection of my body."*

*"I am stunning. I am gorgeous. I love everything about myself."*

Make sure that you keep repeating them throughout the day. It's the nature of the mind to constantly think. You might as well give it something positive and beautiful to hold on to.

Before retiring to bed, write down the affirmations again in your gratitude journal. You can also carry your journal with you all day so that you can give it a quick read whenever you are in need of a confidence boost or a little pep talk from the self.

## Affirmations in Front of the Mirror

How many times have you looked in the mirror and mourned over your flaws? If you are like most women then this is likely a daily routine for you. Now, tell me how many times have you looked in the mirror and appreciated what you see?

I'll suggest that you look in the mirror every morning and night, and appreciate what you see in it. Look into your own eyes and say out aloud, "You are stunning. You are beautiful. I love you for who you are and exactly the way you are."

It might not be easy for you to do this and in the beginning. Your mind might even make you think that you are deceiving yourself but don't give up. Persevere until this becomes your very reality. It takes 21 days to form any new habit so don't give up before three weeks and don't miss even a single day.

Once you become your own greatest admirer and lover, the whole world starts becoming enamored by your presence. I know that you might have a lot of limiting beliefs that will come in the way of you realizing your fabulousness but don't give up.

Appreciating your own beauty might seem vain and self-centered but that's simply because we have been conditioned to believe this. When you see the best in yourself, you also start seeing the best in others. You exude an aura of quiet self-confidence as you no longer expect other people to tell you what you should be thinking about yourself.

A woman who loves herself and is completely confident about who she is makes other people feel at home with who they are. Self-love does not make one narcissistic. It makes one more loving because you can only give what you have for yourself. When you are hypercritical about your own self, you are also hypercritical about others. When you love yourself completely for who you are, you also love others for who they are without wanting to change anything.

**Practice Greater Love and Kindness**

Have you ever noticed how a woman who is in love has a certain glow on her face? Love has that power to make even the plainest of faces appear dazzlingly beautiful. You don't need to be with a man in order to be in love or to be kind. Having love in your heart towards nature and towards all of creation is enough to make you outstandingly beautiful. A beautiful heart always illuminates a lovely face from within.

When you treat anyone with love and kindness, you automatically become more beautiful. Think about this for a second: have you ever come across an outlandishly beautiful woman who when she opened her mouth came across as inconsiderate and unkind. Did she suddenly not become less beautiful?

On the other hand, you met someone who might not be considered conventionally pretty or beautiful but there was an aura of charm around her. There was a certain magnetism that seems to bewitch anyone who comes close to her.

Her behavior, her words, her posture, her grace makes her wildly attractive. She's a woman who knows how to make the most of what she has been born with. However, the thing that matters most to her is that she wants to be like a ray of sunshine in this world so that anyone who comes in her presence becomes automatically uplifted.

Practice being kind to others including to yourself. Instead of thinking constantly about your faults, focus on what you do love about yourself. I would suggest writing down 10 things you love about yourself and posting it at a place where you can see it regularly.

Celebrate who you are by loving yourself for being YOU.

**Poise and Posture**

How you carry your body can dramatically alter your appearance. You must practice sitting, walking and standing in the correct posture. You might have to take deportment classes to get it right though as it's very difficult to learn this by reading a book or by looking at pictures and videos.

Ideally, when you walk, it should appear as if you are gliding like a gentle breeze. Needless to say, while sitting down, legs should always be together. Keeping your legs arranged at an angle to the side creates a more fluid and feminine posture. You can cross them at the ankles to make the posture more comfortable but never cross your legs at your knees. Not only is crossing your legs at the knees bad for your health but it is also, in reality, a more masculine posture as it creates a square or boxy silhouette. If you try out both the postures in the mirror you will see for yourself what I mean. When it comes to the hands, let one hand rest on top of the other in your lap.

The correct posture for standing involves keeping one leg in front of the other and the knees slightly bent. Make sure that you keep your spine erect at all times as if a string was pulling you from the base of your spine through the top of your skull like a puppet.

Again, I would suggest signing up for etiquette and deportment classes to learn the skills in person.

No amount of online instruction can be a substitute for the guidance of a hands-on trainer since you are not going to know your own faults when practicing through online guidance.

I have personally also found ballet classes to be very helpful in developing posture and grace. Even if you have never taken ballet lessons in your life, it's never too late to get started. In fact, there is a lot of research showing that adults can learn ballet better and faster. Usually, this is because someone who decides to take up ballet in adulthood is far more committed to mastering it than children who are doing it out of compulsion.

If you can find a good adult ballet class near you, then I would highly recommend that you get started with it right away. Ballet helps you become more graceful as you learn how to move your body with calculated fluid movements.

If ballet does not interest you, then you can also consider taking up Yoga or Tai Chi. Any form of physical exercise that focuses on slow, gentle and graceful movements of the body will help you develop poise in the long run.

Also, it's not about becoming good at it but to do the best that you can and to truly enjoy the practice. You are doing this for yourself and not to participate in a competition (of course, if at any point you become so passionate about your practices that you'd want to professionally compete, then that's great too!).

## Slow Down a Bit

Have you noticed how some women have a natural aura of elegance? You might think it's their clothes that makes them stand out but I am sure you have come across some women who might not be wearing couture pieces but still manage to look like royalty.

From my own personal observations, I have come to the conclusion that elegance is all about deliberate movement and careful conduct.

What makes one person appear elegant and another not so much depends heavily on the amount of thought one puts into what they are doing and how they are conducting themselves at any given moment.

Therefore, I would say that one of the easiest and most effective ways to become more elegant is to do things slowly and with thought. So if you are walking, walk just a little slowly. Meditate on how your feet are moving. Allow yourself to feel like royalty while you are doing something as banal as crossing the street or walking in the park.

Same goes for every other activity – take the time to eat your food, chewing every morsel slowly, enjoying the gentle release of flavors in your mouth. Talk slowly so that the words coming out of your mouth are clear and infused with deliberate intention. Also, refrain from any kind of gossip or backbiting. Before speaking, always ask yourself if what you are going to speak is kind and helpful or not? Of course, that does not mean you have to agree with everything that is being said or done. You can disagree with things while retaining your composure and keeping your words restrained.

An elegant woman always has a sense of dignity and tremendous self-control. She never allows anyone's words or actions to fester her to an extent that she'd not appear to be in control of herself.

The recipe for becoming elegant and graceful is simple – do everything like a meditation. No matter what the task at hand is, do it with complete involvement of your body, mind and soul. It does not matter how anyone else perceives you because, in reality, you are the most important person in the world to you.

## Treat Yourself as The Most Special Person in the World and Each Day as A Special Occasion

If you were invited to a Red Carpet event would you go there with unkempt hair and in your yoga pants? I'm sure that like most people you'd likely make an effort to look your best.

Every day of your life is special and each day is your very own red Carpet extravaganza.

The problem is that most of us take life for granted. We think that we'd live forever so we don't take the time to make each day special. If you start thinking that this day is the only day you have, you'd probably do things very differently.

I am urging you to live every day of your life as if it was the only day you had. Of course, I am not suggesting that you take out your taffeta evening gown and wear it to the grocery store but that silk blouse which makes you feel like a million bucks – sure, go for it! Even if you wanted to watch Netflix wearing your taffeta evening gown there's really nothing wrong with it though. The point I am trying to make here is that you must stop waiting for that special occasion when you'll dress your best and be your best. Instead, be your best every day and take the time to make your day extra special in every way possible.

This might not be very easy as you might have to deal with other people's curiosity. You might get asked things like, "Oh you are so dressed up. Where are you going?" Dealing with such questions can feel annoying but take them as a compliment. You are setting a positive example by being immaculate in an increasingly sloppy world. Maman taught me that being over-dressed is far better than being underdressed.

When you carry yourself with dignity and care, you are sending out a strong message to the world. You are telling the world who you are and how you want to be treated. If you want to be treated like royalty, then dress the part and act the part every day. Who cares whether you become an actual Duchess or not as long as you get treated like one.

You'll automatically experience a massive change in your outlook and attitude towards life once you start wearing your best clothes on a daily basis. Even on the hardest of days, simply dressing well has the power to uplift our mood and self-confidence. No matter what you are going through in life, never allow yourself to become sloppy. Take the time to take care of yourself and to make yourself feel special because you truly deserve it.

I do all these things myself and I saw my mother live like this so I am talking from a place of experience. If it's possible for me and for my mother, then everything that I have outlined in this chapter is also possible for you. Just remember that how the world treats you is only a magnified reflection of how you see and treat your own self.

Be your own biggest fan and treat yourself with the love and respect that you truly deserve.

## Suggested exercises for Inner Beauty, Elegance and Poise

- Allow yourself to feel beautiful. Constantly remind yourself that you are incredibly beautiful.

- Look in the mirror and tell yourself how beautiful you really are. Focus on your strengths and tell yourself what all you appreciate about yourself.

• Start and end your day with gratitude. Keep your gratitude journal at your bedside. As soon as you wake up, write down 5 things that you are grateful for (make sure that at least 3 of them are small things that you'd easily take for granted. Also, try to come up with something new every day). At the end of the day, write down 5 things that happened in your day or that you have in your life for which you are grateful. Do this exercise even if you are feeling dejected and negative. It will have a strong impact on your mindset and your life. Be sure to do this for at least 21 days as it takes 21 days to form any new habit. Once you have completed the initial 21 days, then, take the vow to do the exercise for another 21 days. You'll soon start loving the process and miracles will also start unfolding in your life.

• Pick 1-2 beauty affirmations that you write down in your gratitude journal every morning and night. You'd also ideally be repeating the affirmations in your mind throughout the day. Let these affirmations replace all negative self-talk and criticism.

• Look in the mirror every morning and night – appreciate what you see in it. Look into your own eyes and say out aloud, "You are stunning. You are beautiful. I love you for who you are and exactly the way you are."

• Write down 10 things you love about yourself and paste it at a place where it would be visible to you.

# Chapter 2

# Create Your Own Custom Beauty Care Schedule

Great skin and gorgeous luscious locks start with basic cleanliness. You must keep yourself immaculately clean at all times. You can buy the most expensive makeup or creams but if your skin is not naturally healthy and clean, then nothing will work for you. In France, there is a lot of emphasis on staying natural by having beautiful skin from within while also using less makeup.

This is very much in contrast to the American approach to beauty. During my stay in the States, I noticed that the emphasis was on covering up the flaws by applying a lot of makeup. Whereas, in France, I don't see women wearing a lot of makeup.

In fact, I never saw Maman wear heavy foundation. She would use a tinted moisturizer or a light liquid foundation to keep her skin hydrated and looking fresh, followed by basic makeup like a dab of powder, blush, mascara, eyeliner and her signature red lipstick.

I personally still follow this regimen. IN France, women are more focused on maintaining the health of their skin by eating fresh healthy food, getting regular sleep and applying the highest quality products that they can afford.

It's crucial to have a beauty care routine for yourself. It is much easier to look well-groomed and presentable 24/7 if you schedule out a little pampering session every day of the week.

In this chapter, I'll give you a sample routine that you can modify to match your personal requirements and lifestyle.

The sample schedule that I am providing here will help you to look your best over the weekends as you'll be doing the beauty care routine throughout the week. This will leave you with plenty of time to spend with your family over the weekends.

You can also clamp 2-3 things together or even have one entire pampering day for yourself. Whatever you do, just make sure that you are taking out ample time to take care of yourself throughout the week. You should be your own greatest priority as you can only give others what you have for yourself. A healthy amount of self-love and self-care goes a long way in boosting one's self-confidence.

## Monday – Give Yourself a Rejuvenating Facial

You can use any organic oil suited to your skin or your favorite moisturizer/cream. Try to do this when you have at least 10-15 minutes for yourself. It will be a good idea to do this before going to bed. You can play your favorite relaxing music in the background to make the experience even more relaxing and soothing.

## What You'll Need:

✓ A gentle face wash
✓ A gentle scrub
✓ Your favorite oil or cream/lotion
✓ A small face towel for steaming your face
✓ Hot Water
✓ Fresh lemon skin and a little heavy whipping cream
✓ Moisturizer/night cream/toner

## Directions:

- Start by removing all makeup and cleaning your face with a gentle face wash. Massage your face thoroughly in gentle circular movements for 5-10 minutes (you can learn about pressure points by referring to books and videos that teach *acupressure facial*. This can be very beneficial in accentuating the benefits you derive from a face massage).

- After the massage, steam your face and extract any blackheads (I'll give you a special beauty secret here that Maman taught me: if you want long-term relief from stubborn blackheads, then take a lemon and squeeze all the juice out of it. Put some heavy whipping cream on one half (turned inside out so that the inner juicy part is exposed completely) and gently rub your nose with the lemon skin for a minute or two. If you do this every day for about a week, you'll notice all the blackheads disappear. Consistency is important here. It's safe enough to do this every day. Make sure that the lemon skin is fresh and soft. The cream also must be fresh).

- After steaming, apply a mask and let it sit on your face for 10-20 minutes. Wash off and apply your favorite moisturizer/toner/night cream.

- The benefit of doing this at night before bedtime is that you will wake up the next day with fresh and rejuvenated skin as the moisturizing products you apply after doing this thorough facial will be absorbed more deeply by the skin. Yet, of course, you can also do the facial in the morning, afternoon or at just about any time that works for you.

However, if you have a choice, then I'd say go for the bedtime facial.

### Tuesday – Time to Give Your Feet Some Love

Your feet carry you everywhere so they certainly deserve some love and attention. It really doesn't require much time to give yourself a nice pedicure. You can do this even while watching TV.

### What you'll need:

✓ A tub of hot water
✓ Some shampoo
✓ 2 tablespoons olive oil
✓ Regular salt or Epsom salt
✓ Your favorite essential oil (optional)

✓ A foot file
✓ Orange stick
✓ Nail clippers
✓ Cuticle pusher
✓ Your favorite nail polish

**Directions:**

- Take a tub of hot water and pour some shampoo in it. Add regular salt or if you have Epsom salt, then throw some of that into the water. You can also add 2 tablespoons of olive oil to moisturize and hydrate your feet along with a few drops of your favorite essential oil.

- After removing the nail polish, soak your feet in this water. For 15-20 minutes, allow yourself to completely relax.

- Thereafter, use the foot file to remove dead skin from each foot. Use the orange stick to clean the nail bed. With the cuticle pusher, you can push the cuticle to give your nail a more defined shape. However, I do not recommend cutting the cuticle as it can make your skin prone to infections. Cuticles are there for a reason after all! Maman would never let me cut them and I don't recommend that you do it either.

- Clip your nails and wash your feet with clean warm water. Pat dry and apply a thick moisturizer.

- Now, it's time to apply the nail polish! I would suggest that you first wipe the nail clean with a nail polish remover to make sure that there is no oil or moisture on the nail before you apply nail polish.

Now, you are ready to put your best foot forward!

**Wednesday - Body Hair and Eyebrows**

I understand that some women are not in favor of removing body hair. This is completely fine but if you are amongst the group who does like to remain fuzz-free, then Wednesday might be a good day to get the job done.

Make sure that you remove body hair from all the areas you like to keep fuz-free using your preferred method. If you need to go to the salon for this, then set up an appointment in advance. I personally like to get a professional body wax once a month. Every week, I do maintenance sessions at home. I am especially particular about keeping my legs fuzz-free since I tend to wear a lot of dresses and skirts. My preferred method is waxing. I like to buy at-home waxing kits that are very easy to use once you have mastered the technique.

Just remember to apply the wax in the direction of hair growth and pull out the strip in the opposite direction. It's certainly a tad painful, but to me, it's worth the pain.

A lot of women prefer to shave their legs and that's fine too. For me, this doesn't work well as I start getting new growth within just a day or two of shaving.

When it comes to eyebrows, I have discovered that tending to them regularly is the best way of maintaining their shape. I prefer to do my eyebrows myself as I am rarely satisfied with the work they do at salons. If you have someone who does the job perfectly for you, then stick with that person I'd say. But if like, me, your eyebrows often go from fab to drab at the hands of another person, then maybe building up a little eyebrow design skills will serve you well.

When it comes to the shape, French women prefer to keep their eyebrows as natural looking as possible so over-plucking, over-arching and over-shaping is completely out of question for most of us.

You must also remember that no two eyebrows are ever exactly alike so don't strive for perfection. Opt for excellence instead.

**Eyebrow Shaping Basics**

In order to shape your eyebrows correctly, imagine a line going up from outside of your nose towards your eyebrows. For the finishing point, imagine a diagonal line drawn from the outer corner of your eyes. The starting point of the brow should be bushier and it should taper down into a softer line.

Use a tweezer to pluck out the extra hair. If you are too confused about the right shape, then I'd suggest drawing a thick line in the shape of your eyebrows using an eyebrow pencil. This way you know that you have to pluck out only those hairs that fall outside of the line. You can use an eyebrow razor or eyebrow wax strips (be very very careful with this. If you are an absolute beginner, then this might not be a good idea) to remove unwanted hairs from the top part of the brows.

For everyday styling, I suggest using an eyebrow powder along with eyebrow wax. From my own personal experience, I have found this to be the best way to keep eyebrows looking well-groomed and natural. I am not a huge fan of eyebrow pencils but some women seem to swear by it.

An eyebrow shaping brush also comes in handy to keep all the hair in the right place and pointed in the direction that best suits your brow shape.

**Thursday – Hair Care**

Give yourself a relaxing head massage, and then shampoo your hair. If you don't have time for a massage, then at least just shampoo your hair. You can follow up with a deep conditioner to provide additional moisture to your hair. I also like to use lemon water to rinse my hair. This provides added shine and makes the scalp feel super clean. All you need to do is add the juice of one lemon to a large glass of water and use it as a final rinse.

Also, be sure to brush your hair well before washing. If you have oiled your hair, then you can avoid this step. Instead, make sure that you brush your hair before oiling it.

For shampooing, dilute a tablespoon of shampoo in 4-5 tablespoons of water and spread it all over your wet hair and scalp. Massage your scalp thoroughly to clean it thoroughly. Rinse your hair and apply a conditioner. Wash off the conditioner and use the lemon water as a final rinse.

Maman taught me right at a very young age that hot water was BAD for hair. You should try to use the coldest temperature that you can tolerate for washing and rinsing your hair. Hot water is severely damaging to hair. It can cause problems like dandruff, hair fall and split ends.

Also, in France, we rarely ever blow dry our hair. I would suggest that you allow your hair to air dry as much as possible. I would also recommend that you master a few heatless hairstyles that can be your go-to everyday styles.

Maman taught me that every woman should have at least one style for leaving her hair loose and at least two updos that she can use for both formal and informal occasions. There are a lot of heatless hairstyles that you can master to look your best.

I would highly recommend that you regularly style your hair so that you become really good at a few. Think about the feeling you get when you walk out of the salon with a fresh head of hair. If you are like most women, then you probably feel like a new person. The confidence boost you get and the sense of having your head in the clouds makes it totally worthwhile to put in the effort for becoming your own celebrity hairstylist.

Again, great hair starts with a clean head of hair so always pay attention to the condition and health of your hair. If you need to shampoo more often, then that is fine too. In fact, I tend to shampoo my hair twice a week. I prefer to wash my hair at least one day before an important event simply because a day old hair tends to have better texture and, therefore, responds better to styling.

This regimen is only meant to be a rough guideline to help you build a schedule that works for you. My purpose here is to remind you of all the self-care elements that combine together to create the most fabulous version of yourself.

### Friday – Time for a Manicure

The reason why I am suggesting Fridays for a manicure is so that you can dive into the weekend using your perfectly manicured hands. Doing it so close to the weekends will ensure that there is minimal chipping and fading of nail color.

I would also suggest that you plan your manicure as the last chore of the night so that you have ample time to let your nails dry completely. Make sure that you don't have any tasks left that will require your hands. Allow the polish to set completely before retiring to bed. If you go to bed too early then you might end up with pesky fiber and fabric imprints on your nails.

Also, I would caution you against using your nails as a digging tool. Nothing proves more disastrous to nail health and beauty than this disastrous practice. Handle your hands with care and gratitude as they help you get so much done!

If you are wondering why you sometimes get white flecks on nails, then let me tell you that they are not because of any vitamin or mineral deficiency. They are mechanical injuries caused to the base of your nails.

I must also mention here that since the palms of your hands and the soles of your feet do not have any sebaceous glands, they require a little extra pampering through daily application of heavy creams suitable for use in these areas.

Now let's get to the DIY manicure.

### What You'll Need:
    ✓ Nail polish remover
    ✓ Warm water

✓ Your favorite shampoo

✓ 2 tablespoons olive oil

✓ A few drops of essential oil (optional)

✓ Nail file (I suggest using a glass file for minimal damage to the nails and best results)

✓ Nail clippers

✓ Cuticle Pusher

✓ Nail Brush

✓ Clean towels

✓ Base coat

✓ Top coat

✓ Your choice of nail polish

**Directions**

- Start by removing the old polish. I like to use an oil-based remover that is acetone free. This protects the nails from the drying effects of acetone and of other strong chemicals.

- Give your hands a quick rinse with plain water and pat them dry. Wait until nails are completely dry. Now, it's time to clip (if you need to) and file your nails. Maman used to say that nails should never be filed while they are damp. This can cause them to split and break. Also, you probably already know this but I'll still repeat: file only in one direction.

- When it comes to the shape and size of the nails, I would suggest sticking to a medium length and a practical shape like an oval or a square. Pointed nails and extremely long nails are very hard to maintain. Unless you are absolutely sure that you want to sport them everyday, I would suggest going for the most practical and least damaging style.

- Soak your nails in warm water to which olive oil, shampoo and essential oils have been added.

- Brush your nails using the nail brush.

- Push your cuticles using the cuticle pusher. I do not recommend cutting the cuticles as this can lead to infections.

- Rinse your hands in plain water and pat dry using the towels. Make sure that there is no oily residue left on your nails. If your nails still feel oily, then wipe them with an acetone-based nail polish remover.

- Apply the base coat to all your nails (wait until the base coat dries completely) followed by two coats of polish. Once the polish has dried completely, apply the top coat for added shine and durability.

Tips: A quick way to refresh your polish during the week is to apply another layer of top coat whenever you feel like your nails are looking dull.

**Saturday and Sunday**
It's time to go out and have fun! You can also obviously brush up on any grooming details that require extra attention.

Just remember that this sample beauty schedule is all about flexibility. The idea is to take some time out every day to take care of your beauty. You also have the alternative of fitting all the activities into one single day but for most women, that's usually quite overwhelming and difficult to maintain over the long-term.

Make grooming an essential part of your daily routine and life will never catch you off-guard. Maman always looked impeccable no matter what was actually going on in her life. It all starts with giving yourself some time for yourself every day!

# Chapter 3

# My French Mother's Best Beauty Tips

➤ Love yourself and don't be afraid to feel gorgeous and amazing all the time (because you really are)!

➤ No matter how demanding your schedule is, always take some time out for yourself. A little self-love goes a long way. When you take care of yourself, you are happier and healthier. A happy and healthy person can take better care of others.

➤ Always sit straight – it's perfectly possible to be completely relaxed while sitting straight. When you are walking, keep your back straight, shoulders relaxed and chest pushed forward. Imagine as if a string is pulling you up from the base of your spine through the top of your head.

➤ Enjoy the food you eat instead of counting calories or being obsessed with fad diets. If you eat your food with joie de vivre and lead an active lifestyle, you will never gain weight.

➤ Love with all your heart and soul. When you are emotionally fulfilled, you are less likely to overeat.

➤ Be passionate about everything you do. A woman who is passionate and loving is always attractive.

➤ Know who you are and what you want to stand up for. Once you know who you are, it's much easier to figure out a wardrobe that represents the values you stand for.

➤ Your greatest love affair should be with yourself. When you love yourself and are completely content with who you are as a person, you are far less likely to seek the approval of others. Such a person commands the respect and admiration of all. You are also much more likely to be successful in relationships as you don't cling on to another person for emotional fulfillment and approval.

➤ Always cook fresh and take your time to eat. Don't be in a hurry. NEVER stand and eat or NEVER eat while walking.

➤ Wear your best lingerie every day (and make sure they are color coordinated) – not because someone needs to see you in it but because you feel amazing and sexy when you know that you are dressed to kill inside out.

➤ Never equate sloppiness with relaxation. You can look relaxed wearing a dressing gown around the house rather than a tattered hoodie and track pants.

➤ Make the effort to look your best but make it appear as if you got up looking like a million bucks.

➤ Red lipstick is like a cherry on the cake. It can make any outfit stand out. It can make you look flawless with just one swipe. So don't hesitate and go for it!

➤ Wear your most comfortable shoes if you are going to be walking around a lot. However, always keep a pair of dressy shoes in your bag just in case you might decide to go somewhere fancy. Shoe bags are truly a life savior and life's too short to be unprepared for anything! Also, keep a pair of nice shoes in your office drawer. Once you get to the office, you can change into them.

➤ Embrace your imperfections and make the most of what nature has given you. French women are usually very content with what they have been born with. While plastic surgery and cosmetic enhancement isn't completely non-existent in France, it is surely not as much of a phenomenon as it is in the US. At the same time, if you really like the idea of getting a little help, then don't hesitate. The most important thing in life is to be true to yourself and to do what makes you happy. Don't let society or someone else dictate to you how you must live your life.

# Chapter 4

# My French Mother's Best Tips for Gorgeous Hair

➤ Master 2 hairstyles that are easy and practical for you. Make sure that at least one of the two hairstyles is an updo. It doesn't have to be anything complicated – a simple French twist that you have nailed down to perfection would get you feeling like a million bucks in a matter of minutes.

➤ In addition to these 2, master 1 fairly complicated looking style (doesn't have to be actually complicated) for special occasions.

➤ Shun the hairdryer. Let your hair air dry as much as possible.

➤ Take a few drops of Argan oil and spread it on your palms. Run your palms through your hair for smoother shinier locks.

➤ Add the juice of one lemon to a glass of water. Use the mixture as your last rinse after shampooing and conditioning.

➤ Use a brush that has a combination of nylon and boar bristles. Maman always said that I must never go to bed without brushing my teeth and removing my makeup. She taught me that the right way to brush my hair was by flipping it upside down and then moving the brush in smooth strokes from scalp to the hair ends.

Later, you flip all your hair back in place and brush the crown of your head in smooth strokes. She advocated doing this ritual every night for a few minutes. In the morning, a quick hair brushing session is good to get you going for the day. I have stuck to this routine through the years.

I think owning a few good hair grooming tools is absolutely essential for maintaining hair health and beauty. The reason why brushing is so important is because it removes a lot of dust and debris that might have accumulated throughout the day. Using a natural bristle brush also ensures that the natural oils get evenly distributed throughout the hair.

➤ Maman also discouraged me from shampooing my hair more than twice a week. She would tell me that shampooing too often strips the hair off all the moisture. It might be difficult to change the habit especially if you are shampooing every day but it's worth making the effort. Daily shampooing can strip your hair off all the natural oils making it limp and brittle. It won't be easy cutting down your shampooing regime as at first, your hair will revolt against it by producing excessive oil. If you can battle this initial stage, then you will have healthier hair in the long-run. While you are stuck in the excess oil-production phase, you can try out a few tricks to make the situation more bearable. Use dry shampoo if you must. In case you have bangs, you can isolate them and shampoo only your bang area.

➤ Wash your hairbrushes every time you shampoo. Clean hairbrushes are just as important as clean hair.

➤ Always keep a small hairbrush in your handbag for a quick fix whenever you need it.

➤ Never skimp on getting a good haircut. Investing in a good stylist is an absolute must if you want to wear your hair with confidence every day.

➤ Apply a natural hair mask at least once a week. You can make your own DIY protein mask by whisking 2 egg whites. Add 2 tablespoons of honey and 1 tablespoon of argan oil to the mixture. Apply this mask to damp towel dried hair.

Cover the hair with a shower cap and let your hair absorb all the nutrition for half an hour. Wash off the mixture with a shampoo. Follow up with a conditioner and a lemon water rinse. Needless to say, let your hair air-dry afterwards!

➤ Embrace your natural hair color as much as possible. If you must color your hair, then stick with a shade that is closest to your natural hair color.

➤ NEVER use hot water to wash hair. It will lead to hair fall, dandruff and split ends.

➤ Brush and detangle your hair before shampooing it. This will loosen the dirt and debris.

➤ Never step out of the house with unstyled wet hair. If you must go out with wet hair, then at least put it up in a sleek chignon.

➤ Invest in good hair care products that are as natural as possible. Steer clear of parabens and SLS laden products.

➤ Sleep on a silk pillowcase or secure your hair in a silk scarf while sleeping.

➤ Find a signature haircut and style that truly flatters your face and stick with it. It might be fun to try out trendy new hairstyles every now and then but sticking with a signature style will minimize chances of a hair disaster.

➤ Be regular with hair trims. Maintaining your haircut is the second most important thing after getting an amazing cut.

# Chapter 5

# My French Mother's Best Tips for Flawless Skin

➤ Stick to natural skin care products as much as possible.

➤ Don't look for quick fixes. Instead, make long-term investments by taking good care of your skin and body.

➤ Organic cold-pressed oils are the best for keeping your skin hydrated and moisturized. I have extremely oily skin that tends to respond best to a combination of hazelnut and calendula oil. In case, you have extremely dry skin, then you can go for a heavy oil like avocado and wheat germ. For normal skin, you can go for a light oil like grapeseed, sweet almond or olive.

➤ NEVER go to bed with any makeup on your face. No matter how tired you are, always remove your makeup and wash your face thoroughly before retiring for the night.

➤ Find a facialist who really understands your skin. Once you have formed a trusting relationship, be sure to get regular facials.

➤ Makeup should blend in with your skin. Use a foundation color that is closest to your natural skin tone. You will likely have to use two-three different shades throughout the year as skin color changes during summer and winter depending upon how tanned or pale your skin is. Don't just stick to one color but always have a few colors handy so that you can find the one that best matches your skin at that point of time.

➤ Use distilled water to which a few drops of your favorite essential oil has been added as a makeup setting spray.

➤ Wash your face with an AHA based face wash. You can easily find a glycolic face wash at the local pharmacy.

➤ Scrub your body with a homemade scrub every 7-10 days. You can make the scrub by mixing 1 cup powdered sugar with 1/4 cup olive oil, the juice of 1 lemon and a few drops of your favorite essential oil (optional). Store the mixture in an airtight jar. Use the mixture in the shower on damp skin. Scrub the skin until all the sugar granules have dissolved. (Caution: Don't use this mixture on your face as it can be too harsh for it)

➤ For the face, stick to gentler exfoliating agents. I would suggest that you start using a retinol based moisturizer/cream at night. You can buy it as an OTC product from the pharmacy or you can ask your dermatologist for a prescription. Retinol is a powerful anti-aging ingredient that increases skin cell turnover, thereby, slowing down the clock for you. It also removes dead skin cells so regular application should help you retain a fresh dewy complexion.

➤ Use sun protection as much as possible. The best kind of sun protection actually involves using physical barriers like an umbrella, a thick scarf, a wide-brimmed hat, etc.

➤ When it comes to sunscreens, it's better to buy sunblocks versus sunscreens. Sunblock needs to be reapplied every 3-4 hours in order to retain its effectiveness. For reapplication purposes, I would suggest keeping a sunblock spray handy.

➤ Always have a few signature lipsticks in pink and red that match your skin tone perfectly. No other lipstick color can make a woman stand out more than the quintessential red lips.

➤ Keep your makeup classic and simple. You should make yourself an adept at doing at least two different look: one for the day, another for special occasions and eveningwear.

The day look should be mild and as close to natural as possible (of course, red lipstick can be worn at any time of the day as it goes really well with just about any makeup look). On the other hand, the evening look should be heavier.

➤ Every woman must have a few signature perfumes. Never buy a perfume by smelling the bottle at a store. Spritz the perfume on your pulse points and test how it lasts through the day. Only if you are completely satisfied with how long it lasts and what it smells like after a few hours, should you proceed with the purchase.

➤ In France, dressing well and looking your best at all times is considered a form of politeness. Therefore, always put your best face forward, even if you are just going around the corner to buy bread. Every day is a special occasion called life. After all, you never know who you might bump into while buying bread at the corner store. You don't want to be unprepared for anything!

➤ Start every meal with a soup or salad. This will not only give you beautiful skin but will also keep your weight in check. Opt for fruit as a dessert whenever you can. However, don't be scared of a little indulgence every now and then. Just remember that it's all about portion control.

# Chapter 6

# My French Mother's Best Tips for Beautiful Nails

➤ Not only is it possible to know the state of your health from the appearance of your nails but it is also possible to find out just how well you treat yourself by looking at them. Therefore, be sure to take excellent care of your nails.

➤ Unlike the US, nail salons are quite rare and much more expensive in France. Most French women tend to their nails themselves. The preferred look is one that is as close to natural as possible. Most French women never get extensions. The preferred nail length is usually somewhere between a short and a medium. When it comes to nail polish colors, classics rule the roost. Shades of nude and red can be seen everywhere. A lot of women prefer to steer clear of polish altogether focusing entirely on clean shiny naturally beautiful nails (some might choose to apply just one coat of clear polish though).

➤ There is nothing French about the 'French Manicure.' In fact, it is quite flashy for most French women's taste. I can swear that I never saw Maman or any of my other female family and friends with it.

➤ Protect your hands and nails while doing housework. Make gloves your best friend. Use a pair of fabric gloves while doing housework that does not require water. Use rubber gloves for all the work that requires water. Use dish scrapers and brushes to clean dishes. Don't ever give in to the temptation of using your nails as a digging tool.

➤ If you must touch any abrasive substance during housework, then make sure that you are touching it with the ball of your fingers and not your nails. Also, apply a generous amount of a heavy hand cream to keep the skin protected.

➤ While drying hands, use the towel to push back the cuticles firmly but gently. This will prevent the development of hangnails.

➤ Use heavy-duty gardening gloves whenever you are tending to your plants and garden.

➤ Clean the nails with a soft bristle nail brush once a day.

➤ Apply a thick layer of hand cream before retiring to bed. Wear fabric gloves for deeper penetration of the cream and also to protect your bed sheets from staining.

➤ It's better to go without polish than to go around with chipped polish. Stick to your weekly manicure schedule in order to keep your nails and hands in top shape.

➤ Maman taught me this amazing tip: Pinch the sides of your nails gently for a few minutes every day in order to change the shape of your nails. It will take 6-8 months to see any real change but you can bring your nails in a perfect almond shape with this method.

# Chapter 7

# How to Take Care of a Chic Wardrobe

Think about the chicest women you have come across – whether in real life or celebrities on screen. If you are observant enough, you'll notice that there is a measured precision in the way they carry themselves. In fact, it won't be an exaggeration to say that most chic women are pretty much an embodiment of neatness. For a 1962 article in the magazine, *Town & Country*, Siriol Hugh-Jones, wrote about Jackie Kennedy, "Her look gives the impression that someone has neatened you up with a sharp razor blade and finished off the whole effect with a small mathematical bow."

You might think that if only you had unlimited money to buy fancy new clothes all the time, you'd look like a million bucks every day. This is only partially true. Indeed, you need high-quality clothes to look and feel your best. However, you don't need to break the bank for that because it's not the quantity of clothes that matters. Instead, looking your best depends entirely on how well you are maintaining your existing wardrobe.

## Taking Care of Your Clothes

Being well-dressed and presentable surely requires you to be more thoughtful about all your choices, especially when you are trying to do it within a specific budget. I would suggest that you must mold your wardrobe according to your unique personal style.

You can refer to my first book, *French Chic – The Ultimate Guide to French Fashion, Beauty and Style*, to understand the basics of building a chic wardrobe.

Most well-dressed women in real life don't change their style often.

They remain true to the style that best represents their personality and creates the persona that they want to project to the world.

Once you have identified your personal style, you'll have to identify the key pieces that contribute to creating such a look. For instance, if your style is feminine and romantic, then you might want to focus on adding blouses or dresses with ruffles, blows, lace and flowery patterns to your wardrobe.

If your style is bohemian, then flowy dresses, geometric prints, oversized T-shirts might fit in better with your wardrobe. This is all about the game of elimination. You have to know exactly what doesn't work for you.

For instance, if you have identified your personal style as feminine and romantic but you go to the store and there is a beautiful blouse with geometric prints on it, you might feel tempted to buy it. But the question you'd have to ask yourself at that point is if it would fit in with the rest of your wardrobe? How likely are you to wear it over and over again? The blouse might be worth only $20 but if you were to wear it only once, the overall cost will be far greater than that of a $100 blouse which might be worn regularly for 3-4 years. The idea here is to think long-term. I also have one important personal strategy here. I don't buy anything I am absolutely sure that I am completely in love with that piece. Usually, I'd check out all the nearby stores and survey what's available there before deciding to buy anything from anywhere.

Of course, this doesn't mean that you can never buy anything that doesn't completely fit into your existing wardrobe. The only thing I'd want you to consider before deciding to buy something that is very new for your existing wardrobe is the fact that you'd likely have to buy other items in order to make the piece blend in with the rest of your look.

Also, instead of going after designers and brand names, go for quality. Sometimes you might be able to find incredibly beautiful high-quality clothing from emerging designers at local boutiques than what you'd find at expensive high-end stores.

Again, being well-dressed is all about a little planning and some proactive steps taken keenly every day. You can establish daily, weekly and monthly rituals to take better care of your wardrobe.

In this chapter, I'll give you a few pointers to help you establish a maintenance routine for your existing wardrobe. Just remember that if you'll take better care of your clothes, your clothes will gladly help you to look your best and most presentable every day.

## Invest in Garment Care

Maman used to say that you need to spend more on garment care than on the garment itself. Now, I realize how true this is. You might have a $200 dress but if you don't take care of in the correct way, then it might end up looking like a frumpy $10 dress.

Therefore, buy the best quality garment care products and services that you can afford to get. In fact, I absolutely don't recommend skimping when buying garment care products. If you think about it, then you'll realize that this is a relatively small investment in the long-run. Your clothes will require fewer trips to the dry cleaners and the cost of getting them professionally mended will also be much less in the long-run.

These are the basic items you'll require to take care of your garments properly. I'd suggest acquiring them at the soonest if you don't already have any of them:

*High-Quality Garment Brushes* (one regular size for use at home and another travel-size for traveling)

A high-quality garment brush is absolutely necessary for keeping your clothes in pristine order. I brush my clothes before hanging them back in the closet and also use the brush to remove any surface dirt, hair or dandruff before heading out of the house. Look at your brush as the finishing touch to any outfit. Use it at the end of your getting dressed ritual.

Make sure that you only buy natural bristle brushes that are gentle enough for your clothes. You might need more than one as special fabrics like silk, cashmere and wool would require gentler care.

Therefore, it is totally worth buying brushes made specifically for use on certain fabrics. A good brush will easily last you a lifetime even with regular use. As far as I can recall, Maman had the same brushes her whole life and so did my father.

## A Garment Steamer

A garment steamer is an absolute must-have in the wardrobe of any well-dressed woman. Using the steamer on clothes that you take off at night but will be wearing again is an excellent way of reviving the freshness of the garment. The best part is that the garment steamer can be used on the clothing while it is still on the hanger.

(I wouldn't recommend this for items that are specifically 'dry clean' only. Using a garment steamer on such clothes might leave moisture spots on them.)

Be sure to take the garment steamer with you while traveling. I personally find this a very handy tool for reviving crushed dresses and blouses while on vacation.

## Washing and Cleaning Supplies

Again, don't skimp on cleaning products. Buy the highest quality products that you can afford to get. Stay away from products with strong chemical-based formulas. Try to buy gentler products that don't have a strong chemical-like odor.

Also, make sure that you are separating your whites from your colored clothes while washing. I also ensure that I am washing my blacks and blues separately as they can attract a lot of lint if thrown in with a regular load. It might also be worth hand washing some of your garments that are too delicate to be thrown into the washing machine.

## High-quality Hangers

How you hang your clothes determines a lot about how well they will retain their shape in the long-run.

You might not want to spend a lot on buying quality hangers, but trust me, having quality hangers in your wardrobe is indispensable if you want to maintain your clothes in mint condition for years.

Now, the question is what kind of hangers should you really buy? Ideally, you should have several different types of hangers in your wardrobe. You'll need shaped wooden hangers for hanging your coats and jackets. For skirts, the best hanger would be the clip type that can hold your skirts upright from both ends of the waistband. Delicate blouses should be hung on thickly padded hangers. Felt-lined clamp hangers are best for hanging pants. You should also have a special hanger designed specifically for hanging scarves and another one designed specifically for hanging belts.

Avoid the urge to hang too many clothes on one hanger. I would highly recommend that you hang each item in your wardrobe separately. Of course, you can fold and store items like tank tops, leggings, and synthetic dresses that don't crease. If you think your wardrobe is too cluttered, then I would suggest doing a closet detox (refer to Book 1 for instructions).

## A Sewing Kit

Even if you think you are an absolute disaster at sewing, I would still advice you to keep a sewing kit handy. Daily inspection of your clothing is the key to remaining immaculately dressed 7 days a week.

Every night after taking off your clothes, inspect your garment – does it need to be put away for washing? Are there stains on it? Are there signs of wear and tear? Has it accumulated dirt, lint or debris?

Take appropriate action immediately. The golden rule for remaining chicly dressed is to only wear clothes that are fresh, neat and in perfect condition.

## *Plan Your Wardrobe in Advance*

Maman would lay out her wardrobe for the next day the previous night itself. I have retained this practice throughout the years. Not only does it save time in the morning but it also ensures that I am not dealing with any last-minute mishaps. I mean just imagine getting ready for a special event only to find out on the last day that there is a big stain in your gorgeous silk dress. I prefer to be prepared well in advance.

For special occasions, I plan my wardrobe at least one week in advance. This way, I have ample time to take care of any stains or signs of wear and tear that my garment might have acquired. This way I also have ample time to get the outfit professionally dry-cleaned.

If you are absolutely incompetent at fixing even minor wear and tear issues with your clothing, I'd suggest it would be worth learning a little bit of basic sewing. If you don't think you have the time and energy for it, then I would suggest that you make good friends with a tailor who can do these tasks for you even on a short notice. No matter what, never wear anything with a stain, a hole, a missing button or any kind of obvious (or not so obvious) defect. That's something I learned from Maman and it's something that I want to pass on to you today.

# Conclusion

Thank you so much for placing your trust in me and for taking this beautiful journey with me! I sincerely hope that I have been able to provide you with something of value that will help you live a chicer life.

Again, I want to remind you that you are beautiful – don't let anyone ever make you feel otherwise. Embrace your own self without judgment and without harsh criticism. It's nice to aspire for self-improvement but the desire to become a better version of yourself must be triggered by self-love and not self-loathing.

I hope you have already tried out most of the suggestions presented in this book. In case you haven't tried them out, then I urge you to start today!

As suggested at the beginning, keep this book as your reference guide for building a more powerful and enjoyable grooming routine. Keep coming back to it and read the ideas over and over again until they are fully internalized into your daily life.

Also, *if you enjoyed this book, then I'd like to ask you for a favor. Would you be kind enough to leave a review for this book on Amazon? It'd be greatly appreciated!*

If you are looking for inspiration to build a **French Chic wardrobe** and you haven't already read the **first book**, then be sure to **check it out**.

If you want to learn more about living a **French Chic lifestyle**, then be sure to check out my **second book**.

Thank you and good luck on your journey to a chicer and more beautiful life!

# Other Books in the French Chic Series

(Available for Purchase on Amazon)

# FRENCH CHIC

## THE ULTIMATE GUIDE TO FRENCH FASHION, BEAUTY AND STYLE

*DRESS CLASSY AND ELEGANT ON ANY BUDGET*

### VERONIQUE ANTOINETTE BLANCHARD

# FRENCH CHIC

## Living

### THE ULTIMATE GUIDE TO A LIFE OF ELEGANCE, BEAUTY AND STYLE

## VERONIQUE ANTOINETTE BLANCHARD

Made in the USA
Middletown, DE
01 May 2020